Cheesecakes

PUBLICATIONS INTERNATIONAL, LTD.

Contents

FAVORITE ALL TIME RECIPES is a trademark of Publications International, Ltd.

Copyright©1989, Kraft, Inc.
All rights reserved.

PHILADELPHIA BRAND and PARKAY are registered trademarks of Kraft, Inc., Glenview, IL 60025.

PILLSBURY'S BEST is a registered trademark of The Pillsbury Co., Minneapolis, MN 55402.

Recipe development and food photography by the Kraft Kitchens.

On the front cover: Marble Cheesecake (see page 22).

On the back cover, clockwise from top right: Miniature Cheesecakes (see page 32), Northwest Cheesecake Supreme (see page 10), Piña Colada Cheesecake (see page 72) and Chocolate Caramel Pecan Cheesecake (see page 14).

ISBN: 0-7853-0061-9

This edition published by:
Publications International, Ltd.
7373 North Cicero Avenue
Lincolnwood, Illinois 60646

Manufactured in U.S.A.

8 7 6 5 4 3 2 1

Superb Cheesecakes

Cheesecakes! Just say the word and you call up visions of sinfully rich, moist, delicious desserts. Almost everyone loves cheesecakes, yet many are intimidated from making cheesecakes at home. Actually, making a cheesecake is very easy. Yes, it takes time to bake, and yes, it takes time to cool and then chill, but putting together the ingredients couldn't be easier. Plus, you have the added benefit of a delicious dessert made well ahead of time, freeing you up to do other things.

What makes a great cheesecake, is, of course, the ingredients. PHILADELPHIA BRAND Cream Cheese is the main ingredient in the cheesecakes offered here. Its fresh, delicate, creamy-smooth flavor is perfect for making marvelous cheesecakes. For over 50 years, Kraft has been developing recipes for cream cheese. One of the first was the "Kraft Philadelphia Cream Cake," published in 1928. This simple cheesecake was an instant success. Since then, the homemade cheesecake has matured and grown as we marble it with chocolate, top it with meringues, garnish it with all manner of fresh fruits and flavor it with everything from peanut butter to liqueurs.

This book offers you two main kinds of cheesecakes to serve to your family and friends. There are traditional baked cheesecakes—a combination of cream cheese, eggs and flavorings poured over a prepared crust, baked for approximately one hour, then cooled and chilled. And then there are no-bake cheesecakes—a combination of unflavored gelatin, cream cheese and flavorings poured over a prepared crust and then simply chilled until set. No-bake cheesecakes tend to be lighter in texture than baked cheesecakes, but both are equally appealing in flavor. Whatever kind of cheesecake you decide to make, consult the next few pages of step-by-step photos. They'll show you just how easy it is to make superb cheesecakes.

Easy Steps Toward a Successful Cheesecake

BAKED

1

For baked cheesecakes, first prepare crust by pressing crust ingredients into pan, in this case a mixture of graham cracker crumbs, sugar and melted margarine. Bake crust while you prepare cheesecake batter.

2

Combine cream cheese and sugar, mixing at medium speed on electric mixer. Beat in eggs, one at a time. For flavored cheesecakes, beat in flavorings, such as melted chocolate shown here.

3

Using a spatula, scrape cheesecake batter into prepared springform pan. Bake for the time given in each recipe. Remove to a wire rack to cool.

4

To loosen cake from rim of springform pan, use a thin metal spatula. Insert spatula between cake and rim of pan; run spatula around inside edge to loosen cake. Allow cheesecake to cool completely.

5

Loosen spring fastener on side of pan. Lift rim of pan straight up to separate it from the cheesecake.

6

Place cheesecake on serving plate and garnish as desired, in this photo, with whipped cream and toasted slivered almonds.

NO-BAKE

7

When making a no-bake cheesecake, combine un-flavored gelatin and cold water in a small saucepan. Let stand until gelatin is softened, about 2 minutes.

8

Heat the softened gelatin over low heat, stirring, until the gelatin is completely dissolved and the mixture is clear.

9

For most recipes, beat softened cream cheese and sugar, mixing at medium speed with electric mixer. Gradually add dissolved gelatin.

10

Chill the cream cheese-gelatin mixture until slightly thickened, but not set. If mixture gels too much, the texture of the finished cheesecake will not be smooth. (If you do overchill the mixture at this point, you can soften it again by dipping bowl in warm water and stirring mixture until slightly softened.)

11

Fold whipped cream and flavoring into chilled cream cheese mixture. Using a circular motion with a spatula, cut down through center of the mixture across bottom of bowl, lifting mixture up and over. Repeat until mixture is well blended.

12

Using same spatula, scrape cream cheese mixture into prepared springform pan. Chill until cheesecake is set, several hours or overnight. To remove cheesecake from springform pan, see photos 4 and 5.

Banana Nut Cheesecake

1 cup chocolate wafer crumbs
¼ cup PARKAY Margarine, melted

Combine crumbs and margarine; press onto bottom of 9-inch springform pan. Bake at 350°, 10 minutes.

2 8-ounce packages PHILADELPHIA BRAND Cream Cheese, softened
½ cup sugar
½ cup mashed ripe banana
2 eggs
¼ cup chopped walnuts

Combine cream cheese, sugar and banana, mixing at medium speed on electric mixer until well blended. Add eggs, one at a time, mixing well after each addition. Stir in walnuts; pour over crust. Bake at 350°, 40 minutes. Loosen cake from rim of pan; cool before removing rim of pan.

⅓ cup milk chocolate pieces
·1 tablespoon PARKAY Margarine
2 teaspoons cold water

Melt chocolate pieces and margarine with water over low heat, stirring until smooth. Drizzle over cheesecake. Chill.

10 to 12 servings

Preparation
time: *25 minutes plus chilling*
Baking time: *40 minutes*

Northwest Cheesecake Supreme

1 cup graham cracker crumbs
3 tablespoons sugar
3 tablespoons PARKAY Margarine, melted

Combine crumbs, sugar and margarine; press onto bottom of 9-inch springform pan. Bake at 325°, 10 minutes.

4 8-ounce packages PHILADELPHIA BRAND Cream Cheese, softened
1 cup sugar
3 tablespoons flour
4 eggs
1 cup sour cream
1 tablespoon vanilla
1 21-ounce can cherry pie filling

Combine cream cheese, sugar and flour, mixing at medium speed on electric mixer until well blended. Add eggs, one at a time, mixing well after each addition. Blend in sour cream and vanilla; pour over crust. Bake at 450°, 10 minutes. Reduce oven temperature to 250°; continue baking 1 hour. Loosen cake from rim of pan; cool before removing rim of pan. Chill. Top with pie filling just before serving.

10 to 12 servings

Preparation
time: *25 minutes plus chilling*

Baking time: *1 hour 10 minutes*

VARIATION *Substitute 1½ cups finely chopped nuts and 2 tablespoons sugar for graham cracker crumbs and sugar in crust.*

Orange-Butterscotch Cheesecake

1¼ cups old fashioned or quick oats, uncooked
¼ cup packed brown sugar
2 tablespoons flour
¼ cup PARKAY Margarine, melted

Combine oats, brown sugar, flour and margarine; press onto bottom of 9-inch springform pan. Bake at 350°, 15 minutes.

3 8-ounce packages PHILADELPHIA BRAND Cream Cheese, softened
¾ cup granulated sugar
2 teaspoons grated orange peel
1 teaspoon vanilla
4 eggs

Combine cream cheese, granulated sugar, peel and vanilla, mixing at medium speed on electric mixer until well blended. Add eggs, one at a time, mixing well after each addition; pour over crust. Bake at 325°, 1 hour and 5 minutes. Loosen cake from rim of pan; cool before removing rim of pan.

½ cup packed brown sugar
⅓ cup light corn syrup
¼ cup PARKAY Margarine, melted
1 teaspoon vanilla

Combine brown sugar, corn syrup and margarine in saucepan; bring to boil, stirring constantly. Remove from heat; stir in vanilla. Chill until slightly thickened. Spoon over cheesecake. Garnish with orange slice and fresh mint, if desired.

10 to 12 servings

Preparation
time: *35 minutes plus chilling*
Baking time: *1 hour 5 minutes*

Chocolate Caramel Pecan Cheesecake

2 cups vanilla wafer crumbs
6 tablespoons PARKAY Margarine, melted

Combine crumbs and margarine; press onto bottom of 9-inch springform pan. Bake at 350°, 10 minutes.

1 14-ounce bag KRAFT Caramels
1 5-ounce can evaporated milk
1 cup chopped pecans, toasted
2 8-ounce packages PHILADELPHIA BRAND Cream Cheese, softened
½ cup sugar
1 teaspoon vanilla
2 eggs
½ cup semi-sweet chocolate pieces, melted

In 1½-quart heavy saucepan, melt caramels with milk over low heat, stirring frequently, until smooth. Pour over crust. Top with pecans. Combine cream cheese, sugar and vanilla, mixing at medium speed on electric mixer until well blended. Add eggs, one at a time, mixing well after each addition. Blend in chocolate; pour over pecans. Bake at 350°, 40 minutes. Loosen cake from rim of pan; cool before removing rim of pan. Chill. Garnish with whipped cream and additional finely chopped pecans, if desired.

10 to 12 servings

Preparation
time: *35 minutes plus chilling*
Baking time: *40 minutes*

Pumpkin Marble Cheesecake

1½ cups gingersnap crumbs
½ cup finely chopped pecans
⅓ cup PARKAY Margarine, melted

Combine crumbs, pecans and margarine; press onto bottom and 1½ inches up sides of 9-inch springform pan. Bake at 350°, 10 minutes.

2 8-ounce packages PHILADELPHIA BRAND Cream Cheese, softened
¾ cup sugar
1 teaspoon vanilla
3 eggs
1 cup canned pumpkin
¾ teaspoon cinnamon
¼ teaspoon ground nutmeg

Combine cream cheese, ½ cup sugar and vanilla, mixing at medium speed on electric mixer until well blended. Add eggs, one at a time, mixing well after each addition. Reserve 1 cup batter. Add remaining sugar, pumpkin and spices to remaining batter; mix well. Spoon pumpkin and cream cheese batters alternately over crust; cut through batters with knife several times for marble effect. Bake at 350°, 55 minutes. Loosen cake from rim of pan; cool before removing rim of pan. Chill.

10 to 12 servings

Preparation
time: *25 minutes plus chilling*
Baking time: *55 minutes*

Chocolate Orange Supreme Cheesecake

1 cup chocolate wafer crumbs
¼ teaspoon cinnamon
3 tablespoons PARKAY Margarine, melted

Combine crumbs, cinnamon and margarine; press onto bottom of 9-inch springform pan. Bake at 325°, 10 minutes.

4 8-ounce packages PHILADELPHIA BRAND Cream Cheese, softened
¾ cup sugar
4 eggs
½ cup sour cream
1 teaspoon vanilla
½ cup semi-sweet chocolate pieces, melted
2 tablespoons orange flavored liqueur
½ teaspoon grated orange peel

Combine cream cheese and sugar, mixing at medium speed on electric mixer until well blended. Add eggs, one at a time, mixing well after each addition. Blend in sour cream and vanilla. Blend chocolate into 3 cups batter; blend liqueur and peel into remaining batter. Pour chocolate batter over crust. Bake at 350°, 30 minutes. Reduce oven temperature to 325°. Spoon remaining batter over chocolate layer; continue baking 30 minutes. Loosen cake from rim of pan; cool before removing rim of pan. Chill. Garnish with chocolate curls, if desired.

10 to 12 servings

Preparation
time: *25 minutes plus chilling*
Baking time: *1 hour*

Citrus Fruit Cheesecake

1 cup graham cracker crumbs
⅓ cup packed brown sugar
¼ cup PARKAY Margarine, melted

Combine crumbs, brown sugar and margarine; press onto bottom of 9-inch springform pan. Bake at 325°, 10 minutes.

4 8-ounce packages PHILADELPHIA BRAND Cream Cheese, softened
1 cup granulated sugar
4 eggs
2 tablespoons shredded orange peel
Assorted fresh fruit

Combine cream cheese and granulated sugar, mixing at medium speed on electric mixer until well blended. Add eggs, one at a time, mixing well after each addition. Blend in peel; pour over crust. Bake at 325°, 50 minutes. Loosen cake from rim of pan; cool before removing rim of pan. Chill. Top with fruit. Garnish with lime peel, if desired.

10 to 12 servings

Preparation
time: *20 minutes plus chilling*
Baking time: *50 minutes*

Marble Cheesecake

1 cup graham cracker crumbs
3 tablespoons sugar
3 tablespoons PARKAY Margarine, melted

Combine crumbs, sugar and margarine; press onto bottom of 9-inch springform pan. Bake at 350°, 10 minutes.

3 8-ounce packages PHILADELPHIA BRAND Cream Cheese, softened
¾ cup sugar
3 tablespoons flour
1 teaspoon vanilla
3 eggs
1 1-ounce square unsweetened chocolate, melted

Combine cream cheese, sugar, flour and vanilla, mixing at medium speed on electric mixer until well blended. Add eggs, one at a time, mixing well after each addition. Blend chocolate into 1 cup batter. Spoon plain and chocolate batters alternately over crust; cut through batters with knife several times for marble effect. Bake at 450°, 10 minutes. Reduce oven temperature to 250°; continue baking 30 minutes. Loosen cake from rim of pan; cool before removing rim of pan. Chill.

10 to 12 servings

Preparation
    time: *20 minutes plus chilling*
Baking time: *40 minutes*

Carrot & Raisin Cheesecake

1 cup graham cracker crumbs
3 tablespoons granulated sugar
½ teaspoon cinnamon
3 tablespoons PARKAY Margarine, melted

Combine crumbs, granulated sugar, cinnamon and margarine; press onto bottom of 9-inch springform pan. Bake at 325°, 10 minutes.

3 8-ounce packages PHILADELPHIA BRAND Cream Cheese, softened
½ cup granulated sugar
½ cup flour
4 eggs
¼ cup KRAFT 100% Pure Unsweetened Orange Juice
1 cup finely shredded carrot
¼ cup raisins
½ teaspoon ground nutmeg
¼ teaspoon ground ginger

Combine 2½ packages cream cheese, granulated sugar and ¼ cup flour, mixing at medium speed on electric mixer until well blended. Add eggs, one at a time, mixing well after each addition. Blend in juice. Add combined remaining flour, carrots, raisins and spices; mix well. Pour over crust. Bake at 450°, 10 minutes. Reduce oven temperature to 250°; continue baking 55 minutes. Loosen cake from rim of pan; cool before removing rim of pan. Chill.

1 tablespoon KRAFT 100% Pure Unsweetened Orange Juice
1 cup sifted powdered sugar

Combine remaining cream cheese and juice, mixing until well blended. Gradually add powdered sugar, mixing until well blended. Spread over top of cheesecake. Garnish with additional raisins and finely shredded carrot, if desired.

10 to 12 servings

Preparation
     time: *30 minutes plus chilling*
Baking time: *1 hour 5 minutes*

Chocolate Chip Cheesecake Supreme

1 cup chocolate wafer crumbs
3 tablespoons PARKAY Margarine, melted

Combine crumbs and margarine; press onto bottom of 9-inch springform pan. Bake at 350°, 10 minutes.

3 8-ounce packages PHILADELPHIA BRAND Cream Cheese, softened
¾ cup sugar
¼ cup flour
3 eggs
½ cup sour cream
1 teaspoon vanilla
1 cup mini semi-sweet chocolate pieces

Combine cream cheese, sugar and flour, mixing at medium speed on electric mixer until well blended. Add eggs, one at a time, mixing well after each addition. Blend in sour cream and vanilla. Stir in chocolate pieces; pour over crust. Bake at 325°, 55 minutes. Loosen cake from rim of pan; cool before removing rim of pan. Chill. Garnish with whipped cream and fresh mint, if desired.

10 to 12 servings

Preparation
time: *20 minutes plus chilling*
Baking time: *55 minutes*

Caramel-Apple Sundae Cheesecake

⅓ cup PARKAY Margarine
⅓ cup sugar
1 egg
1¼ cups flour

Beat margarine and sugar until light and fluffy. Blend in egg. Add flour; mix well. Spread dough onto bottom and sides of 9-inch springform pan. Bake at 450°, 10 minutes.

2 8-ounce packages PHILADELPHIA BRAND Cream Cheese, softened
⅔ cup sugar
2 tablespoons flour
3 eggs
½ cup sour cream
1 cup peeled, chopped apple
¾ teaspoon cinnamon
½ cup KRAFT Caramel Topping
¼ cup chopped pecans

Combine cream cheese, ⅓ cup sugar and flour, mixing at medium speed on electric mixer until well blended. Add eggs, one at a time, mixing well after each addition. Blend in sour cream. Toss apples in remaining sugar and cinnamon. Stir into cream cheese mixture. Pour over crust. Swirl ¼ cup caramel topping into cream cheese mixture. Bake at 350°, 1 hour. Loosen cake from rim of pan; cool before removing rim of pan. Chill. Top with remaining caramel topping and pecans.

10 to 12 servings

Preparation
time: *25 minutes plus chilling*

Baking time: *1 hour*

Regal Cranberry Cheesecake

1 cup graham cracker crumbs
3 tablespoons sugar
3 tablespoons PARKAY Margarine, melted

Combine crumbs, sugar and margarine; press onto bottom of 9-inch springform pan. Bake at 325°, 10 minutes.

3 8-ounce packages PHILADELPHIA BRAND Cream Cheese, softened
¾ cup sugar
2 tablespoons flour
2 teaspoons vanilla
3 eggs
1 cup sour cream
1 cup cranberry orange sauce, chilled

Combine cream cheese, sugar, flour and vanilla, mixing at medium speed on electric mixer until well blended. Add eggs, one at a time, mixing well after each addition. Blend in sour cream; pour over crust. Bake at 450°, 10 minutes. Reduce oven temperature to 250°; continue baking 30 minutes. Loosen cake from rim of pan; cool before removing rim of pan. Chill. Spoon sauce over cheesecake. Garnish with orange peel and fresh mint, if desired.

10 to 12 servings

Preparation
time: *20 minutes plus chilling*

Baking time: *40 minutes*

VARIATIONS *Substitute 10-ounce container frozen cranberry orange relish, thawed, for cranberry orange sauce.*

Substitute Light PHILADELPHIA BRAND Neufchâtel Cheese for Cream Cheese.

Miniature Cheesecakes

⅓ cup graham cracker crumbs
1 tablespoon sugar
1 tablespoon PARKAY Margarine, melted

Combine crumbs, sugar and margarine. Press rounded measuring tablespoonful of crumb mixture onto bottom of each of six paper-lined muffin cups. Bake at 325°, 5 minutes.

1 8-ounce package PHILADELPHIA BRAND Cream Cheese, softened
¼ cup sugar
1½ teaspoons lemon juice
½ teaspoon grated lemon peel
¼ teaspoon vanilla
1 egg
KRAFT Apricot, Cherry or Strawberry Preserves

Combine cream cheese, sugar, juice, peel and vanilla, mixing at medium speed on electric mixer until well blended. Blend in egg; pour over crust, filling each cup ¾ full. Bake at 325°, 25 minutes. Cool before removing from pan. Chill. Top with preserves just before serving.

6 servings

Preparation
time: *20 minutes plus chilling*

Baking time: *25 minutes*

VARIATION *Substitute fresh fruit for KRAFT Preserves.*

MAKE AHEAD *Wrap chilled cheesecakes individually in plastic wrap; freeze. Let stand at room temperature 40 minutes before serving.*

Cappuccino Cheesecake

1½ cups finely chopped nuts
2 tablespoons sugar
3 tablespoons PARKAY Margarine, melted

Combine nuts, sugar and margarine; press onto bottom of 9-inch springform pan. Bake at 325°, 10 minutes.

4 8-ounce packages PHILADELPHIA BRAND Cream Cheese, softened
1 cup sugar
3 tablespoons flour
4 eggs
1 cup sour cream
¼ cup cold water
1 tablespoon instant coffee granules
¼ teaspoon cinnamon

Combine cream cheese, sugar and flour, mixing at medium speed on electric mixer until well blended. Add eggs, one at a time, mixing well after each addition. Blend in sour cream. Bring water to boil. Add coffee granules and cinnamon; stir until dissolved. Cool; gradually add to cream cheese mixture, mixing until well blended. Pour over crust. Bake at 450°, 10 minutes. Reduce oven temperature to 250°; continue baking 1 hour. Loosen cake from rim of pan; cool before removing rim of pan. Chill. Garnish with whipped cream and whole coffee beans, if desired.

10 to 12 servings

Preparation
    time: *25 minutes plus chilling*
Baking time: *1 hour 10 minutes*

Luscious White Chocolate Cheesecake

1½ cups (18) crushed creme-filled chocolate cookies
3 tablespoons PARKAY Margarine, melted

Combine crumbs and margarine; press onto bottom of 9-inch springform pan. Bake at 350°, 10 minutes.

3 8-ounce packages PHILADELPHIA BRAND Cream Cheese, softened
½ cup sugar
½ teaspoon vanilla
3 eggs
½ pound white chocolate, melted

Combine cream cheese, sugar and vanilla, mixing at medium speed on electric mixer until well blended. Add eggs, one at a time, mixing well after each addition. Blend in white chocolate; mix well. Pour over crust. Bake at 350°, 40 minutes. Loosen cake from rim of pan; cool before removing rim of pan. Chill. Garnish with apricot rose and lemon leaves, if desired.

10 to 12 servings

Preparation
time: *20 minutes plus chilling*

Baking time: *40 minutes*

To Make Apricot Rose

Place 6 dried apricot halves between two sheets of wax paper; roll flat with rolling pin. Roll 1 apricot into a cone; arrange remaining apricots around cone to form rose. Loosen outer apricots slightly to "open" rose. Secure bottom with wooden picks to hold shape. Freeze 20 minutes. Cut off bottom to form flat base. Remove wooden picks; brush rose with 2 teaspoons corn syrup.

Chocolate Raspberry Cheesecake

1½ cups (18) finely crushed creme-filled chocolate cookies
2 tablespoons PARKAY Margarine, melted

Combine crumbs and margarine; press onto bottom of 9-inch springform pan.

4 8-ounce packages PHILADELPHIA BRAND Cream Cheese, softened
1¼ cups sugar
3 eggs
1 cup sour cream
1 teaspoon vanilla
1 6-ounce package semi-sweet chocolate pieces, melted
⅓ cup strained KRAFT Red Raspberry Preserves

Combine 3 packages cream cheese and sugar, mixing at medium speed on electric mixer until well blended. Add eggs, one at a time, mixing well after each addition. Blend in sour cream and vanilla; pour over crust. Combine remaining package cream cheese and melted chocolate, mixing at medium speed on electric mixer until well blended. Add preserves; mix well. Drop rounded measuring tablespoonfuls of chocolate cream cheese batter over plain cream cheese batter; do not swirl. Bake at 325°, 1 hour and 20 minutes. Loosen cake from rim of pan; cool before removing rim of pan.

1 6-ounce package semi-sweet chocolate pieces
¼ cup whipping cream

Melt chocolate pieces with whipping cream over low heat, stirring until smooth. Spread over cheesecake. Chill. Garnish with additional whipped cream, raspberries and fresh mint, if desired.

10 to 12 servings

Preparation
  time: *30 minutes plus chilling*
Baking time: *1 hour 20 minutes*

Amaretto Peach Cheesecake

3 tablespoons PARKAY Margarine
⅓ cup sugar
1 egg
¾ cup flour

Beat margarine and sugar until light and fluffy. Blend in egg. Add flour; mix well. Spread dough onto bottom of 9-inch springform pan. Bake at 450°, 10 minutes.

3 8-ounce packages PHILADELPHIA BRAND Cream Cheese, softened
¾ cup sugar
3 tablespoons flour
3 eggs
1 16-ounce can peach halves, drained, pureed
¼ cup almond flavored liqueur

Combine cream cheese, sugar and flour, mixing at medium speed on electric mixer until well blended. Add eggs, one at a time, mixing well after each addition. Add peaches and liqueur; mix well. Pour over crust. Bake at 450°, 10 minutes. Reduce oven temperature to 250°; continue baking 1 hour and 5 minutes. Loosen cake from rim of pan; cool before removing rim of pan. Chill. Garnish with toasted almond slices and additional peach slices, if desired.

10 to 12 servings

Preparation
time: *25 minutes plus chilling*
Baking time: *1 hour 15 minutes*

Mint Chocolate Candy Cheesecake

1 cup chocolate wafer crumbs
3 tablespoons PARKAY Margarine, melted

Combine crumbs and margarine; press onto bottom of 9-inch springform pan. Bake at 350°, 10 minutes.

3 8-ounce packages PHILADELPHIA BRAND Cream Cheese, softened
⅔ cup sugar
3 eggs
1 6-ounce package semi-sweet chocolate pieces, melted
½ cup chopped creme de menthe mint wafers
½ cup sour cream
1 teaspoon vanilla

Combine cream cheese and sugar, mixing at medium speed on electric mixer until well blended. Add eggs, one at a time, mixing well after each addition. Blend in chocolate, mint wafers, sour cream and vanilla; pour over crust. Bake at 350°, 50 minutes. Loosen cake from rim of pan; cool before removing rim of pan. Chill. Garnish with additonal mint wafers, if desired.

10 to 12 servings

Preparation
time: *20 minutes plus chilling*
Baking time: *50 minutes*

Boston Cream Cheesecake

1 9-ounce package yellow cake mix

Grease bottom of 9-inch springform pan. Prepare cake mix as directed on package; pour batter evenly into springform pan. Bake at 350°, 20 minutes.

2 8-ounce packages PHILADELPHIA BRAND Cream Cheese, softened
½ cup granulated sugar
1 teaspoon vanilla
2 eggs
⅓ cup sour cream

Combine cream cheese, granulated sugar and vanilla, mixing at medium speed on electric mixer until well blended. Add eggs, one at a time, mixing well after each addition. Blend in sour cream; pour over cake layer. Bake at 350°, 35 minutes. Loosen cake from rim of pan; cool before removing rim of pan.

2 tablespoons cold water
2 1-ounce squares unsweetened chocolate
3 tablespoons PARKAY Margarine
1 cup powdered sugar
1 teaspoon vanilla

Bring water to boil; remove from heat. Melt chocolate with margarine over low heat, stirring until smooth. Remove from heat. Add water and remaining ingredients; mix well. Spread over cheesecake. Chill several hours. Garnish with strawberries, if desired.

10 to 12 servings

Preparation
    time: *25 minutes plus chilling*
Baking time: *55 minutes*

Lattice Cherry Cheesecake

1 20-ounce package PILLSBURY'S BEST Refrigerated Sugar Cookies

Slice dough into ⅛-inch slices. Arrange slices, slightly overlapping, on bottom and sides of greased 9-inch springform pan. With lightly floured fingers, seal edges to form crust.

2 8-ounce packages PHILADELPHIA BRAND Cream Cheese, softened
1 cup sour cream
¾ cup sugar
¼ teaspoon almond extract
3 eggs
1 21-ounce can cherry pie filling

Combine cream cheese, sour cream, sugar and extract, mixing at medium speed on electric mixer until well blended. Add eggs, one at a time, mixing well after each addition. Reserve ¼ cup batter; chill. Pour remaining batter over crust. Bake at 350°, 1 hour and 10 minutes. Increase oven temperature to 450°. Spoon pie filling over cheesecake. Spoon reserved batter over pie filling in criss-cross pattern to form lattice design. Bake at 450°, 10 minutes. Loosen cake from rim of pan; cool before removing rim of pan. Chill.

10 to 12 servings

Preparation
    time: *25 minutes plus chilling*

Baking time: *1 hour 20 minutes*

VARIATION *Substitute 13 x 9-inch baking pan for 9-inch springform pan. Prepare recipe as directed except for baking. Bake at 350°, 40 minutes. Increase oven temperature to 450°. Continue as directed.*

Cheesecake Germania

1 cup chocolate wafer crumbs
2 tablespoons sugar
3 tablespoons PARKAY Margarine, melted

Combine crumbs, sugar and margarine; press onto bottom of 9-inch springform pan. Bake at 325°, 10 minutes.

3 8-ounce packages PHILADELPHIA BRAND Cream Cheese, softened
¾ cup sugar
¼ cup cocoa
2 teaspoons vanilla
3 eggs

Combine cream cheese, sugar, cocoa and vanilla, mixing at medium speed on electric mixer until well blended. Add eggs, one at a time, mixing well after each addition. Pour over crust. Bake at 350°, 35 minutes. Loosen cake from rim of pan; cool before removing rim of pan. Chill.

⅓ cup evaporated milk
⅓ cup sugar
¼ cup PARKAY Margarine
1 egg, beaten
½ teaspoon vanilla
½ cup chopped pecans
½ cup flaked coconut

In small saucepan, combine milk, sugar, margarine, egg and vanilla; cook, stirring constantly, until thickened. Stir in pecans and coconut; cool. Spread on cheesecake.

10 to 12 servings

Preparation
     time: *25 minutes plus chilling*
Baking time: *35 minutes*

Hollywood Cheesecake

1 cup graham cracker crumbs
3 tablespoons sugar
3 tablespoons PARKAY Margarine, melted

Combine crumbs, sugar and margarine; press onto bottom of 9-inch springform pan. Bake at 325°, 10 minutes.

2 8-ounce packages PHILADELPHIA BRAND Cream Cheese, softened
½ cup sugar
1 tablespoon lemon juice
1 teaspoon grated lemon peel
½ teaspoon vanilla
2 eggs, separated

Combine cream cheese, sugar, juice, peel and vanilla, mixing at medium speed on electric mixer until well blended. Add egg yolks, one at a time, mixing well after each addition. Beat egg whites until stiff; fold into cream cheese mixture. Pour over crust. Bake at 300°, 45 minutes.

1 cup sour cream
2 tablespoons sugar
1 teaspoon vanilla

Combine sour cream, sugar and vanilla. Carefully spread over cheesecake; continue baking 10 minutes. Loosen cake from rim of pan; cool before removing rim of pan. Chill. Garnish with strawberry halves or KRAFT Strawberry Preserves, if desired.

10 to 12 servings

Preparation
    time: *20 minutes plus chilling*
Baking time: *55 minutes*

Cocoa-Nut Meringue Cheesecake

1 7-ounce package flaked coconut, toasted
¼ cup chopped pecans
3 tablespoons PARKAY Margarine, melted

Combine coconut, pecans and margarine; press onto bottom of 9-inch springform pan.

2 8-ounce packages PHILADELPHIA BRAND Cream Cheese, softened
⅓ cup sugar
3 tablespoons cocoa
2 tablespoons cold water
1 teaspoon vanilla
3 eggs, separated

Combine cream cheese, sugar, cocoa, water and vanilla, mixing at medium speed on electric mixer until well blended. Blend in egg yolks; pour over crust. Bake at 350°, 30 minutes. Loosen cake from rim of pan; cool before removing rim of pan.

Dash of salt
1 7-ounce jar KRAFT Marshmallow Creme
½ cup chopped pecans

Beat egg whites and salt until foamy; gradually add marshmallow creme, beating until stiff peaks form. Sprinkle pecans on cheesecake to within ½ inch of outer edge. Carefully spread marshmallow creme mixture over top of cheesecake to seal. Bake at 350°, 15 minutes. Cool.

10 to 12 servings

Preparation
time: *25 minutes plus chilling*
Baking time: *45 minutes*

Greek-Style Cheesecake

PARKAY Margarine
3 8-ounce packages PHILADELPHIA BRAND Cream Cheese, softened
½ cup sugar
2 tablespoons flour
3 eggs
½ cup plain yogurt
½ teaspoon grated lemon peel

Line bottom of 9-inch springform pan with wax paper. Lightly grease sides of pan with margarine. Combine cream cheese, sugar and flour, mixing at medium speed on electric mixer until well blended. Add eggs, one at a time, mixing well after each addition. Blend in yogurt and peel. Pour into prepared pan. Bake at 325°, 50 minutes. Loosen cake from rim of pan; cool before removing rim of pan. Chill.

⅓ cup honey
1 tablespoon PARKAY Margarine

Combine honey and margarine in small saucepan. Bring to boil over medium heat, stirring constantly. Continue boiling 1 minute. Cool to spreading consistency. Spread over chilled cheesecake just before serving. Garnish with lemon peel and fresh mint, if desired.

10 to 12 servings

Preparation
    time: *25 minutes plus chilling*
Baking time: *50 minutes*

Autumn Cheesecake

1 cup graham cracker crumbs
3 tablespoons sugar
½ teaspoon cinnamon
¼ cup PARKAY Margarine, melted

Combine crumbs, sugar, cinnamon and margarine; press onto bottom of 9-inch springform pan. Bake at 350°, 10 minutes.

2 8-ounce packages PHILADELPHIA BRAND Cream Cheese, softened
½ cup sugar
2 eggs
½ teaspoon vanilla

Combine cream cheese and sugar, mixing at medium speed on electric mixer until well blended. Add eggs, one at a time, mixing well after each addition. Blend in vanilla; pour over crust.

4 cups thin peeled apple slices
⅓ cup sugar
½ teaspoon cinnamon
¼ cup chopped pecans

Toss apples with combined sugar and cinnamon. Spoon apple mixture over cream cheese layer; sprinkle with chopped pecans. Bake at 350°, 1 hour and 10 minutes. Loosen cake from rim of pan; cool before removing rim of pan. Chill.

10 to 12 servings

Preparation
    time: *25 minutes plus chilling*

Baking time: *1 hour 10 minutes*

VARIATION *Add ½ cup finely chopped pecans with crumbs for crust. Continue as directed.*

Coconut Choco Cheesecake

1 cup graham cracker crumbs
3 tablespoons sugar
3 tablespoons PARKAY Margarine, melted

Combine crumbs, sugar and margarine. Press onto bottom of 9-inch springform pan. Bake at 350°, 10 minutes.

2 1-ounce squares unsweetened chocolate
2 tablespoons PARKAY Margarine
2 8-ounce packages PHILADELPHIA BRAND Cream Cheese, softened
1¼ cups sugar
¼ teaspoon salt
5 eggs
1 3½-ounce can flaked coconut

Melt chocolate and margarine over low heat, stirring until smooth. Cool. Combine cream cheese, sugar and salt, mixing at medium speed on electric mixer until well blended. Add eggs, one at a time, mixing well after each addition. Blend in chocolate mixture and coconut; pour over crust. Bake at 350°, 1 hour.

1 cup sour cream
2 tablespoons sugar
2 tablespoons brandy

Combine sour cream, sugar and brandy; carefully spread over cheesecake. Bake at 300°, 5 minutes. Loosen cake from rim of pan; cool before removing rim of pan. Chill. Garnish with chocolate shavings, if desired.

10 to 12 servings

Preparation
    time: *25 minutes plus chilling*
Baking time: *1 hour 5 minutes*

Black Forest Cheesecake Delight

1 cup chocolate wafer crumbs
3 tablespoons PARKAY Margarine, melted

Combine crumbs and margarine; press onto bottom of 9-inch springform pan. Bake at 350°, 10 minutes.

2 8-ounce packages PHILADELPHIA BRAND Cream Cheese, softened
⅔ cup sugar
2 eggs
1 6-ounce package semi-sweet chocolate pieces, melted
¼ teaspoon almond extract

Combine cream cheese and sugar, mixing at medium speed on electric mixer until well blended. Add eggs, one at a time, mixing well after each addition. Blend in chocolate and extract; pour over crust. Bake at 350°, 45 minutes. Loosen cake from rim of pan; cool before removing rim of pan. Chill.

1 21-ounce can cherry pie filling
Frozen whipped topping, thawed

Top cheesecake with pie filling and whipped topping just before serving.

10 to 12 servings

Preparation
time: *20 minutes plus chilling*

Baking time: *45 minutes*

Sun-Sational Cheesecake

1 cup graham cracker crumbs
3 tablespoons sugar
3 tablespoons PARKAY Margarine, melted

Combine crumbs, sugar and margarine; press onto bottom of 9-inch springform pan. Bake at 325°, 10 minutes.

3 8-ounce packages PHILADELPHIA BRAND Cream Cheese, softened
1 cup sugar
3 tablespoons flour
2 tablespoons lemon juice
1 tablespoon grated lemon peel
½ teaspoon vanilla
4 eggs (1 separated)

Combine cream cheese, sugar, flour, juice, peel and vanilla, mixing at medium speed on electric mixer until well blended. Add three eggs, one at a time, mixing well after each addition. Beat in remaining egg white; reserve yolk for glaze. Pour over crust. Bake at 450°, 10 minutes. Reduce oven temperature to 250°; continue baking 30 minutes. Loosen cake from rim of pan; cool before removing rim of pan.

¾ cup sugar
2 tablespoons cornstarch
½ cup cold water
¼ cup lemon juice

Combine sugar and cornstarch in saucepan; stir in water and juice. Cook, stirring constantly, until clear and thickened. Beat reserved egg yolk in small bowl. Add small amount of hot mixture to yolk. Return to mixture in saucepan; cook 3 minutes, stirring constantly. Cool slightly. Spoon over cheesecake; chill. Garnish with lemon and lime slices and fresh mint, if desired.

10 to 12 servings

Preparation
  time: *35 minutes plus chilling*
Baking time: *40 minutes*

Heavenly Dessert Cheesecake

1 tablespoon graham cracker crumbs
1 cup low fat (1% to 2%) cottage cheese
2 8-ounce packages *Light* PHILADELPHIA BRAND Neufchâtel Cheese, softened
⅔ cup sugar
2 tablespoons flour
3 eggs
2 tablespoons skim milk
¼ teaspoon almond extract or vanilla

Lightly grease bottom of 9-inch springform pan. Dust bottom with crumbs; remove excess. Place cottage cheese in blender container. Cover; process on high speed until smooth. In large mixing bowl of electric mixer, combine cottage cheese, neufchâtel cheese, sugar and flour, mixing at medium speed until well blended. Add eggs, one at a time, mixing well after each addition. Blend in milk and extract; pour into pan. Bake at 325°, 45 to 50 minutes or until center is almost set. (Center of cheesecake appears soft but firms upon cooling.) Loosen cake from rim of pan; cool before removing rim of pan. Chill. Garnish with raspberries, strawberries or blueberries and fresh mint, if desired.

10 to 12 servings

Preparation
    time: *15 minutes plus chilling*

Baking time: *50 minutes*

VARIATION *Prepare pan as directed; omit blender method. Place cottage cheese in large bowl of electric mixer; beat at high speed until smooth. Add neufchâtel cheese, sugar and flour, mixing at medium speed until well blended. Continue as directed.*

Brownie Swirl Cheesecake

1 8-ounce package brownie mix

Grease bottom of 9-inch springform pan. Prepare basic brownie mix as directed on package; pour batter evenly into springform pan. Bake at 350°, 15 minutes.

2 8-ounce packages PHILADELPHIA BRAND Cream Cheese, softened
½ cup sugar
1 teaspoon vanilla
2 eggs
1 cup milk chocolate pieces, melted

Combine cream cheese, sugar and vanilla, mixing at medium speed on electric mixer until well blended. Add eggs, one at a time, mixing well after each addition. Pour over brownie layer. Spoon melted chocolate over cream cheese mixture; cut through batter with knife several times for marble effect. Bake at 350°, 35 minutes. Loosen cake from rim of pan; cool before removing rim of pan. Chill. Garnish with whipped cream and maraschino cherries, if desired.

10 to 12 servings

Preparation
time: *25 minutes plus chilling*
Baking time: *35 minutes*

Peanut Butter and Jelly Cheesecake

1 cup graham cracker crumbs
3 tablespoons sugar
3 tablespoons PARKAY Margarine, melted

Combine crumbs, sugar and margarine; press onto bottom of 9-inch springform pan. Bake at 325°, 10 minutes.

2 8-ounce packages PHILADELPHIA BRAND Cream Cheese, softened
1 cup sugar
½ cup chunk style peanut butter
3 tablespoons flour
4 eggs
½ cup milk
½ cup KRAFT Grape Jelly

Combine cream cheese, sugar, peanut butter and flour, mixing at medium speed on electric mixer until well blended. (Batter will be very stiff.) Add eggs, one at a time, mixing well after each addition. Blend in milk; pour over crust. Bake at 450°, 10 minutes. Reduce oven temperature to 250°; continue baking 40 minutes. Loosen cake from rim of pan; cool before removing rim of pan. Stir jelly until smooth; drizzle over cheesecake in lattice design. Chill.

10 to 12 servings

Preparation
time: *30 minutes plus chilling*

Baking time: *50 minutes*

VARIATION *Substitute 1 cup old fashioned or quick oats, uncooked, ¼ cup chopped peanuts and 3 tablespoons packed brown sugar for graham cracker crumbs and sugar in crust.*

Chocolate Velvet Cheesecake

1 cup vanilla wafer crumbs
½ cup chopped pecans
3 tablespoons granulated sugar
¼ cup PARKAY Margarine, melted

Combine crumbs, pecans, granulated sugar and margarine; press onto bottom of 9-inch springform pan. Bake at 325°, 10 minutes.

2 8-ounce packages PHILADELPHIA BRAND Cream Cheese, softened
½ cup packed brown sugar
2 eggs
1 6-ounce package semi-sweet chocolate pieces, melted
3 tablespoons almond flavored liqueur

Combine cream cheese and brown sugar, mixing at medium speed on electric mixer until well blended. Add eggs, one at a time, mixing well after each addition. Blend in chocolate and liqueur; pour over crust. Bake at 325°, 35 minutes.

2 cups sour cream
2 tablespoons granulated sugar

Increase oven temperature to 425°. Combine sour cream and granulated sugar; carefully spread over cheesecake. Bake at 425°, 10 minutes. Loosen cake from rim of pan; cool before removing rim of pan. Chill. Garnish with chocolate leaves, if desired.

10 to 12 servings

Preparation
time: *20 minutes plus chilling*

Baking time: *45 minutes*

VARIATION *Substitute 2 tablespoons milk and ¼ teaspoon almond extract for almond flavored liqueur.*

To Make Chocolate Leaves

Wash and dry lemon or rose leaves. Brush leaves with melted semi-sweet chocolate pieces; chill. Carefully peel back leaves from chocolate.

Piña Colada Cheesecake

PARKAY Margarine
1 cup vanilla wafer crumbs
½ cup finely chopped nuts
2 tablespoons sugar
3 tablespoons PARKAY Margarine, melted

Grease sides of 9-inch springform pan with margarine. Combine crumbs, nuts, sugar and margarine; press onto bottom of pan.

1 envelope unflavored gelatin
¼ cup cold water
1 8-ounce package PHILADELPHIA BRAND Cream Cheese, softened
½ cup sugar
1 8-ounce can crushed pineapple
Rum
1 cup whipping cream, whipped
¼ cup toasted coconut

Soften gelatin in water; stir over low heat until dissolved. Combine cream cheese and sugar, mixing at medium speed on electric mixer until well blended. Drain pineapple, reserving liquid. Add enough rum to reserved liquid to measure ¾ cup. Gradually add gelatin and combined rum mixture to cream cheese, mixing until blended. Chill until mixture is thickened but not set. Fold in whipped cream and pineapple; pour over crust. Chill until firm. Sprinkle with coconut.

8 servings

Preparation
time: *25 minutes plus chilling*

Creamy Chilled Cheesecake

1 cup graham cracker crumbs
¼ cup sugar
¼ cup PARKAY Margarine, melted

Combine crumbs, sugar and margarine; press onto bottom of 9-inch springform pan.

1 envelope unflavored gelatin
¼ cup cold water
1 8-ounce package PHILADELPHIA BRAND Cream Cheese, softened
½ cup sugar
¾ cup milk
¼ cup lemon juice
1 cup whipping cream, whipped
Strawberry halves

Soften gelatin in water; stir over low heat until dissolved. Combine cream cheese and sugar, mixing at medium speed on electric mixer until well blended. Gradually add gelatin, milk and juice, mixing until blended. Chill until slightly thickened; fold in whipped cream. Pour over crust; chill until firm. Top with strawberries just before serving.

8 servings

Preparation
time: *25 minutes plus chilling*

Heavenly Orange Cheesecake

1 cup chocolate wafer crumbs
3 tablespoons PARKAY Margarine, melted

Combine crumbs and margarine; press onto bottom of 9-inch springform pan. Bake at 350°, 10 minutes. Cool.

1 envelope unflavored gelatin
½ cup KRAFT 100% Pure Unsweetened Orange Juice
3 8-ounce packages PHILADELPHIA BRAND Cream Cheese, softened
¾ cup sugar
1 cup whipping cream, whipped
2 teaspoons grated orange peel

Soften gelatin in juice; stir over low heat until dissolved. Combine cream cheese and sugar, mixing at medium speed on electric mixer until well blended. Gradually add gelatin mixture, mixing until blended. Chill until slightly thickened; fold in whipped cream and peel. Pour over crust. Chill until firm. Garnish with orange slices and fresh mint, if desired.

10 to 12 servings

Preparation
   time: *25 minutes plus chilling*

Rocky Road Cheesecake

1 cup chocolate wafer crumbs
3 tablespoons PARKAY Margarine, melted

Combine crumbs and margarine; press onto bottom of 9-inch springform pan. Bake at 350°, 10 minutes. Cool.

1 envelope unflavored gelatin
¼ cup cold water
2 8-ounce containers Soft PHILADELPHIA BRAND Cream Cheese
¾ cup sugar
⅓ cup cocoa
½ teaspoon vanilla
2 cups KRAFT Miniature Marshmallows
1 cup whipping cream, whipped
½ cup chopped nuts

Soften gelatin in water; stir over low heat until dissolved. Combine cream cheese, sugar, cocoa and vanilla, mixing at medium speed on electric mixer until well blended. Gradually add gelatin, mixing until blended. Fold in remaining ingredients; pour over crust. Chill until firm. Garnish with additional miniature marshmallows, if desired.

10 to 12 servings

Preparation
time: *25 minutes plus chilling*

Peppermint Cheesecake

1 cup chocolate wafer crumbs
3 tablespoons PARKAY Margarine, melted

Combine crumbs and margarine; press onto bottom of 9-inch springform pan. Bake at 350°, 10 minutes. Cool.

1 envelope unflavored gelatin
¼ cup cold water
2 8-ounce containers Soft PHILADELPHIA BRAND Cream Cheese
½ cup sugar
½ cup milk
¼ cup crushed peppermint candy
1 cup whipping cream, whipped
2 1.65-ounce milk chocolate candy bars, finely chopped

Soften gelatin in water; stir over low heat until dissolved. Combine cream cheese and sugar, mixing at medium speed on electric mixer until well blended. Gradually add gelatin, milk and peppermint candy, mixing until blended. Chill until slightly thickened. Fold in whipped cream and chocolate; pour over crust. Chill until firm. Garnish with additional whipped cream combined with crushed peppermint candy, if desired.

10 to 12 servings

Preparation
time: *25 minutes plus chilling*

Gala Apricot Cheesecake

2¼ cups quick oats, uncooked
⅓ cup packed brown sugar
3 tablespoons flour
⅓ cup PARKAY Margarine, melted

Combine oats, brown sugar, flour and margarine; press onto bottom and 1½ inches up sides of 9-inch springform pan. Bake at 350°, 15 minutes. Cool.

1 envelope unflavored gelatin
⅓ cup cold water
2 8-ounce packages PHILADELPHIA BRAND Cream Cheese, softened
½ cup granulated sugar
2 tablespoons brandy
½ cup finely chopped dried apricots
1 cup whipping cream, whipped

Soften gelatin in water; stir over low heat until dissolved. Combine cream cheese and granulated sugar, mixing at medium speed on electric mixer until well blended. Gradually add gelatin and brandy to cream cheese mixture, mixing until blended. Chill until slightly thickened; fold in apricots and whipped cream. Pour onto crust; chill until firm.

1 10-ounce jar KRAFT Apricot Preserves
1 tablespoon brandy

Heat combined preserves and brandy over low heat; cool. Spoon over cheesecake just before serving.

10 to 12 servings

Preparation
time: *30 minutes plus chilling*

VARIATION *Substitute Light PHILADELPHIA BRAND Neufchâtel Cheese for Cream Cheese.*

Very Smooth Cheesecake

1 cup graham cracker crumbs
3 tablespoons sugar
3 tablespoons PARKAY Margarine, melted

Combine crumbs, sugar and margarine; press onto bottom of 9-inch springform pan. Bake at 325°, 10 minutes. Cool.

1 envelope unflavored gelatin
¼ cup cold water
1 8-ounce package PHILADELPHIA BRAND Cream Cheese, softened
½ cup sugar
1 10-ounce package frozen strawberries, thawed
  Milk
1 cup whipping cream, whipped

Soften gelatin in water; stir over low heat until dissolved. Combine cream cheese and sugar, mixing at medium speed on electric mixer until well blended. Drain strawberries, reserving liquid. Add enough milk to liquid to measure 1 cup. Gradually add combined milk mixture and gelatin to cream cheese, mixing until blended. Chill until slightly thickened. Fold in whipped cream and strawberries; pour over crust. Chill until firm. Garnish with additional whipped cream, sliced strawberries and fresh mint, if desired.

10 to 12 servings

Preparation
time: *25 minutes plus chilling*

VARIATION *Substitute 1 cup vanilla wafer crumbs, ½ cup chopped nuts, 2 tablespoons sugar and 2 tablespoons margarine for graham cracker crumbs, sugar and margarine in crust.*

Cookies and Cream Cheesecake

2 cups (24) crushed creme-filled chocolate cookies
6 tablespoons PARKAY Margarine, softened

Combine crumbs and margarine; press onto bottom and 1½ inches up sides of 9-inch springform pan.

  1 envelope unflavored gelatin
¼ cup cold water
  1 8-ounce package PHILADELPHIA BRAND Cream Cheese, softened
½ cup sugar
¾ cup milk
  1 cup whipping cream, whipped
1¼ cups (10) chopped creme-filled chocolate cookies

Soften gelatin in water; stir over low heat until dissolved. Combine cream cheese and sugar, mixing at medium speed on electric mixer until well blended. Gradually add gelatin and milk, mixing until blended. Chill until mixture is thickened but not set. Fold in whipped cream. Reserve 1½ cups cream cheese mixture; pour remaining cream cheese mixture over crust. Top with chopped cookies and reserved cream cheese mixture. Chill until firm.

8 servings

Preparation
    time: *25 minutes plus chilling*

Holiday Eggnog Cheesecake

1 cup graham cracker crumbs
¼ cup sugar
¼ teaspoon ground nutmeg
¼ cup PARKAY Margarine, melted

Combine crumbs, sugar, nutmeg and margarine; press onto bottom of 9-inch springform pan.

1 envelope unflavored gelatin
¼ cup cold water
1 8-ounce package PHILADELPHIA BRAND Cream Cheese, softened
¼ cup sugar
1 cup eggnog
1 cup whipping cream, whipped

Soften gelatin in water; stir over low heat until dissolved. Combine cream cheese and sugar, mixing at medium speed on electric mixer until well blended. Gradually add gelatin and eggnog, mixing until blended. Chill until slightly thickened; fold in whipped cream. Pour over crust; chill until firm. Garnish with additional whipped cream and nutmeg, if desired.

10 to 12 servings

Preparation
time: *25 minutes plus chilling*

VARIATION *Increase sugar to ⅓ cup. Substitute milk for eggnog. Add 1 teaspoon vanilla and ¾ teaspoon rum extract. Continue as directed.*

Lime Delicious Cheesecake

1¼ cups zwieback toast crumbs
2 tablespoons sugar
⅓ cup PARKAY Margarine, melted

Combine crumbs, sugar and margarine; press onto bottom of 9-inch springform pan. Bake at 325°, 10 minutes. Cool.

1 envelope unflavored gelatin
¼ cup cold water
3 eggs, separated
¼ cup lime juice
½ cup sugar
1½ teaspoons grated lime peel
2 8-ounce packages *Light* PHILADELPHIA BRAND Neufchâtel Cheese, softened
Few drops green food coloring (optional)
2 cups thawed frozen whipped topping

Soften gelatin in water; stir over low heat until dissolved. Beat egg yolks; blend into dissolved gelatin with juice, ¼ cup sugar and peel. Cook, stirring constantly, over medium heat 5 minutes. Cool. Gradually add gelatin mixture to neufchâtel cheese, mixing at medium speed on electric mixer until blended. Stir in food coloring. Beat egg whites until foamy; gradually add remaining sugar, beating until stiff peaks form. Fold egg whites and whipped topping into neufchâtel cheese mixture; pour over crust. Chill until firm. Garnish with lime slices and fresh mint, if desired.

10 to 12 servings

Preparation
time: *25 minutes plus chilling*

VARIATIONS *Substitute lemon juice and grated lemon peel for lime juice and lime peel.*

Substitute PHILADELPHIA BRAND Cream Cheese for Neufchâtel Cheese.

Very Blueberry Cheesecake

1½ cups vanilla wafer crumbs
¼ cup PARKAY Margarine, melted

Combine crumbs and margarine; press onto bottom of 9-inch springform pan. Chill.

1 envelope unflavored gelatin
¼ cup cold water
2 8-ounce packages PHILADELPHIA BRAND Cream Cheese, softened
1 tablespoon lemon juice
1 teaspoon grated lemon peel
1 7-ounce jar KRAFT Marshmallow Creme
1 8-ounce container (3 cups) frozen whipped topping, thawed
2 cups blueberries, pureed

Soften gelatin in water; stir over low heat until dissolved. Gradually add gelatin to cream cheese, mixing at medium speed on electric mixer until blended. Blend in juice and peel. Beat in marshmallow creme; fold in whipped topping and blueberries. Pour over crust. Chill until firm. Garnish with additional thawed frozen whipped topping and lemon peel, if desired.

10 to 12 servings

Preparation
time: *25 minutes plus chilling*

VARIATIONS *Substitute* Light PHILADELPHIA BRAND *Neufchâtel Cheese for Cream Cheese.*

Substitute raspberries or strawberries for blueberries.

Festive Irish Cream Cheesecake

1 cup graham cracker crumbs
¼ cup sugar
¼ cup PARKAY Margarine, melted

Combine crumbs, sugar and margarine; press onto bottom of 9-inch springform pan.

1 envelope unflavored gelatin
½ cup cold water
3 eggs, separated
1 cup sugar
2 8-ounce packages PHILADELPHIA BRAND Cream Cheese, softened
2 tablespoons cocoa
2 tablespoons bourbon
1 cup whipping cream, whipped

Soften gelatin in water; stir over low heat until dissolved. Beat egg yolks; blend into dissolved gelatin with ¾ cup sugar. Cook, stirring constantly, over low heat 3 minutes. Combine cream cheese and cocoa, mixing at medium speed on electric mixer until well blended. Gradually add gelatin mixture and bourbon, mixing until blended. Chill until thickened but not set. Beat egg whites until foamy; gradually add remaining sugar, beating until stiff peaks form. Fold egg whites and whipped cream into cream cheese mixture; pour over crust. Chill until firm. Garnish with chocolate curls and small silver candy balls, if desired.

10 to 12 servings

Preparation
time: *25 minutes plus chilling*

VARIATION *Substitute 2 tablespoons cold coffee for bourbon.*

Recipe Index